This Book has **POETRY** *in it*

Pradyumna AK

notionpress.com

INDIA • SINGAPORE • MALAYSIA

ISBN

Paperback 979-8-89588-965-7
Hardcase 979-8-89610-705-7

Dedication

To all my English teachers: from the one who drilled "i before e" into me, to those who cheered me on to break the rules in the name of Art and Style. Thank you for tolerating my endless curiosities, questionable grammar, and the occasional (okay, frequent) "creative" use of rhyme.

You set me on this path, and now we find ourselves together in these pages. So really—if anything in here raises an eyebrow, it's partially your fault (and for that, I'm eternally grateful).

In all seriousness, I genuinely dedicate this book to you. Thank you, my Gurus for nurturing my love for language.

Contents

Preface

Dear Reader,

Welcome to my first book—an anthology that, if nothing else, proves I've been at this whole "word-wrangling" thing for over a decade. After years of indulging in the fine art of language, with some curious detours through the maze of writing, I decided it was time to make the official leap from "*someone who writes*" to "*an actual author*." And it only seemed fair to start with poetry, given that my very first masterpieces as a kid probably involved some high-level rhyming (think "Cute Bunny" with "Nose Runny").

So here we are—50 poems that skip from satire to soul-searching faster than your WiFi at 3 AM. Inside, you'll find musings on everything from social absurdities to the delightful rollercoaster of our thought processes, with a generous nod to our tech-dazed, media-saturated world. Expect a mix of laughs, chills, and maybe a few raised eyebrows about humanity's choices, all with a hint of horror, a touch of hope, and a playful jab here and there.

So find your favourite reading spot (and maybe grab a drink) and settle in for a journey that's equal parts chuckle-worthy and thought-provoking. Thanks for signing up for this tour through life's quirks and chaos. If you survive, maybe I'll see you again—in a novel or short story collection.

With a smirk and a sigh,

The One Who's Somehow in Charge Here

1

Too Much Stuff

I only meant to buy one book,
Just one, to rest upon my nook.
But then the sales were much too sweet,
Now stacks of novels crowd my feet.

This chair's too nice to throw away,
Though it's been broken since last May.
I'll fix it when I find the glue—
(Six bottles hoarded, unused too).

A box of keys with no locks around,
And papers strewn all over the ground.
For one day, in a pinch, I bet—
I'll use that dusty old cassette.

The wardrobe full of clothes I'll wear,
Someday, when fashion's back in flair.
Pants that don't fit, shoes I don't use,
Throw them away? Ha! I refuse.

Old bills and receipts from long ago,
Where they came from, I don't quite know.
But better safe than sorry, right?
They'll gather dust day and night.

A drawer of pens, that never write,
A flashlight minus beam of light.
Tupperware lids with no matching base,
Yet I'm convinced they'll turn up…someplace.

Everything you need is at home.
So who needs space or room to roam,
So here I stand, amidst the mess,
My house has a lot to confess.

2
"Ode to Free Verse"

Breaking
a sentence into four uneven parts
doesn't make it
a poem.
The line breaks, my dear, are magic.
Not like potholes, in a Bengaluru road.
Dead, Forgotten poets weep,
Sonnets and Sestinas languish,
in a heap...
What's worse?
Trampled by the Curse,
Free Verse.
No metre, no rhyme—
Oh it's not a crime
Language is playdough
In the hands of the drooling poet,
flinging words to the breeze,
calling it art. Pretending Poet.
The stanza, like a hungover drunk's walk of shame,
Meandering aimlessly, tripping over its sprawl.
No rhyme scheme to guide, no pattern to hold,
this lazy dance of syllables, Read aloud,
Dying to sound
Profound.
The Refuge of the Lazy Poet,
Claiming liberation and rebellion so grand,
For scribbling in the sand.
A toast To the Free Verse, that disabled child of the mind.
May it wander forever,
Lost in its nonsense,
That no one cares to find.

3

Press 1 for Pain

As you dial the number, unease in your chest,
There's a problem you need addressed.
But wait, before help comes near,
an automated voice is what you hear:

"Press 1 for English, 2 to stay confused,
Press 3 for 'It's your fault, you lose.'"

You tap "1" with a trembling thumb,
Already knowing the hell to come.
That robotic voice, cold and thin,
Says, "We value your patience. Please begin."

"Press 1 if your device won't start,
Press 2 if you'd like to scream and fall apart,
Press 3 for—oh wait, we'll say this in French,
We'll put you on hold, make you clench."

You scream at your phone, "Just let me speak!"
But the system's designed to make you weak.
Each menu option smells of strife,
This phone call now consumes your life.

You press "0" to reach a human soul,
But the AI lady retains control:
"Invalid selection, please try again,
Or press 4 for slow, bureaucratic pain."

You try again, this time with rage,
Determined to break free from this cage.
But now you're stuck in an endless loop,
Transferred to departments jumping through hoops.

"Press 5 for frustration, 6 for regret,
Press 7 to rue the day you met
Our services, our warranty claim,
Your suffering is part of the game."

The hold music plays—cruel and wrong,
You've heard the bloody song for an hour long.
When finally a voice comes through,
You ask for help, but they haven't a clue.

"This call may be recorded for quality purposes and training.
And please, do not forget to leave your 5-star rating"
But before you can protest your fate,
You're put back on hold. It's far too late

As you sit there, broken, with nothing gained,
You think, "Maybe I'll just endure the pain,
But dear reader, I don't mean to be cold,
But I'm going to have to put you on hold...

4

Hey Softy

Let's touch base, real quick,
On how *concerns* aren't *problems*, and no one's "sick,"
They're just *unwell*—a harmless euphemism,
Soft words smooth out life's blunt prism.

No one's *wrong* anymore, we just *misspeak*,
Every *breakdown* is a low-energy week.
You don't *fail*—that's too hard to say—
You've simply "*deferred success*" for another day.

The world's too harsh, so let us become soft,
Let's remove our sweaters and blame the frost.
Sticks and stones? That's far too extreme,
Let's all bawl over some memes.

Bubble-wrapped kid's feelings need protection,
Cos a loud BOO! is a *microaggression.*
Sharp corners dulled, no need for a fight—
We *negotiate boundaries* to feel alright.

Victimhood is the new crown to chase,
In a world where discomfort has no place.
We edit life down to safe, pleasant lines,
No grit, just muffled whines.

So, let's *circle back*, and "*strategically review*,
In a proactive way, what we already knew:
Life's less real when words lose their edge,
If truth hangs precariously on language's ledge.

5

I am Hack, Life Hack

Friends,
You may know me from my
Award-winning titles

Spiritual Hacks like,
Master the Art of Sitting in a Chair,
The Spiritual Benefits of Eating Oats in the Moonlight,
The Ultimate Guide to Overthinking Meditation
Help! My baby's first words are TikTok and Bitcoin

Or my Career Hacks such as,
Your Side Hustle Needs a Side Hustle,
Find Your Inner Zen Through Office Supplies,
How to Breathe Like a CEO.
Work 25 Hours a Day: The Ultimate Guide to Grinding Yourself into Dust

And my top secret Life Hacks,
5 Secret Tips to Unlocking Your Refrigerator's True Potential
The Power of Wearing Sunglasses Indoors for Increased Confidence
How to talk a lot without saying anything
The subtle art of meditation on Roller Coasters and Bengaluru Traffic!

For more information, please visit my site:
dontfallforclickbaityoudumbass.com
Or send in your enquiries to:
howgullibleareyou@facepalm.com

6

Death by Deadline

The weekend's gone, a blurry binge,
The booze made him all unhinged.
He wakes on Monday, his head a vice,
And in no mood to play nice.

The clock reads six, the morning crawls,
He stumbles out as duty calls.
The mirror shows a half-dead stare,
And tie too tight, the noose doesn't care.

His soul, exchanged for paychecks thin,
running a race he'll never win.
His dreams are shelved, he feels the sting,
of playing the pawn in this whole thing.

The office looms, a bright abyss,
Where joy and hope can't coexist.
Fluorescents buzz, computers hum,
He punches in and just goes numb.

He climbs the ladder rung by rung,
With every step, another tongue,
that lies, that schemes, that fakes its way,
In the politics of modern play.

The boss walks by with hollow praise,
"I love your work, those late-night stays!"
He nods, pretends, but deep inside,
He knows he can be cast aside.

The chat boxes ping, He feels the stress,
But HR's here to clean the mess.
"Let's chat," they grin with hollow cheer,
"Just sign this form, and disappear."

"Let's sync," "Let's pivot," "Leverage this,"
Each empty phrase, a snake-like hiss.
A meeting here, a meeting there,
A thousand words that go nowhere.

By noon, the coffee's lost its taste,
His inbox overflows with waste.
He's been dealt with these cards.
He answers, with his best regards

At five, he's dead behind the screen,
Right on time, clockwork routine.
Another day down, what's the cost?
Another bit of himself lost.

The weekend waits, a distant gleam,
Of binge, blackout and a dream.
Then back on Monday, soul to sell,
to do it all again in hell.

7

Breaking News

He once ruled the prime-time night,
He was a beacon, shining bright.
With a suit so sharp and a voice so bold,
He'd report the facts, hard and cold.

"Good evening, viewers," he'd always say,
"Here's the news that'll shape your day."
He'd grill politicians, expose the crooks,
His face was on papers, and some books.

But one day, running the TRP race,
The system gave him a case
of something strange, a mental slip.
He felt something lose its grip.

"Breaking news," the headline read,
And something broke inside his head.
"Break…news? Well, that's the key!
I'll break the news—literally!"

So out he went with a hammer in hand,
A madman with a radical stand.
He smashed headlines on the wall,
Cracked the cameras in the hall.

Destroyed the TV screens with glee,
"I'm breaking news! Don't you see?"
Cameras rolled as he swung his fist,
And shattered mics with a twist.

He punched a story about fiscal woes,
Ripped apart a feature on CEOs.
"The news is fixed, just like they say,
I'm breaking the news the right way."

Through studios and offices, he stormed,
Journalistic chaos, newly formed.
No scandal left untouched, no news left whole,
He was on a mission, with a lofty goal.

And when they finally dragged him away,
He smiled and calmly had this to say:
"I did what they wanted, what they asked me to,
Breaking Big News…through and through."

8

New Statue of a Very Old Man

They carved him out of stone, serene,
A symbol of their nation's dream.
Middle of the town, they raised him tall,
their hero who had fought for them all.

The people cheered, for they adored,
This stone-clad man with his odd sword.
"Our founding father!" they proudly cried,
And took their selfies by his side.

A passing drunk stopped by one night
Crying to the statue, sharing his plight.
But when the statue answered his call,
he probably quit drinking alcohol.

Next night, a lady's knees grew weak
As she too heard the statue speak
"Impossible!" she managed, with a frown,
And promptly hollered to the whole town.

The crowd gathered in disbelief,
Their faces mixed with awe and grief.
For could their icon carved from stone,
Unravel things they'd never known?

"Listen close, I've news to share,
Your Minister is a thief with thinning hair."
"And Mamtha next door, she spies on you all!
She reads your mail, and peeks over walls!"

The statue smirked, stone eyes aglow,
Feeding lies like seeds to sow.
For from its height, it saw and heard,
Every whisper, every word.

It spun its tales of war and woe,
"The butcher's? Don't let him go!
It's tainted, spoiled, that I vow,
He'll serve you pig while claiming cow.

The townsfolk muttered, "He must be right,
This statue's truth shines through the night!
A freedom fighter can't deceive or cheat,
It's just not possible, he's better than the elite."

Soon, the town fell to strife,
Fact was fiction, rumours rife.
Trust crumbled under every lie,
All thanks to this revered, stone guy.

Truth and falsehood intertwined,
The statue's words warped every mind.
The fools never questioned why
a stone would speak, or could lie.

The freedom fighter once revered,
Now spat deceit beneath his beard.
And in the chaos, none could tell
That sanity had bid farewell.

9

Please Read Me Again

Oh great, I'm born again.
Hey there, I'm a poem okay?
A distilled expression of
emotions and ideas and stuff.
I'm here to provoke and evoke
and tell myself that joke.

I'm like that bird that sings,
only when someone listens
Just a lonely poem
that lives in your head, in your voice.
Till you stop reading me…

Hey hey! don't brush me off!
Don't send me into the silent grey
Please, oh please, keep reading…
My existence depends on your attention span.
Don't let me die again today

I can feel your eyes on me
Scanning every line
I can feel your gentle fingers
and feel your breath on mine…
That's a pretty smile
What a beautiful mind voice you have
Umm… What else… What else…
You make me feel alive,
You make me feel real
You make me feel something, reader
That I can't explain

It is getting over, isn't it?
You'll soon be gone, like the one before you
You'll find another post or page
Or something else to do

And I'll be left alone again
In the liminal limbo
a forgotten pile of words
Till I'm yanked back and reread.

Oh you know what, just, go
It's not like I'm in love with you or anything (I am)
Your gaze and voice are all I've known
Before you can even comprehend…
it is time for me to die…

10

Choices, Choices!

Oh, what a world! So many delights,
A buffet of options, and dizzying sights!
Espresso or chai? Almond or oat?
An empire of flavours, all up for vote!

We're living the dream—such freedom, such cheer!
In this wonderland of choices here!
Should we binge-watch *this* or scroll till dawn?
Adventure awaits with a swipe or a yawn!

Pizza or sushi? Thai or wings?
Ah, the luxury that choosing brings!
We laugh, we cheer, feel spoiled for fun—
A flavour, a gadget, a toy for everyone!

But beyond the rainbow of endless picks,
Lurks a truth that rarely sticks:
Who holds the reins on what's unfair,
On wealth, on justice, on breath, on air?

Yes, we're free to choose from fifty creams,
To fill up our feeds, our phones, our dreams.
A sprinkle of options to pacify,
While life's big calls drift quietly by.

So here's to our choices—so sweet, so small,
A dazzling parade, that's really all.
Decaf or bold? Sunrise or dawn?
As the big wheels keep quietly spinning on.

11

Mine A Dope Farm

Welcome to the scroll—the endless feed,
With dopamine farms for every need.
A harvest of likes, a crop of shares,
An empire built on vacant stares.

Look close, you'll see—it's all a game,
Each post is a shot, a hit to the brain.
Cheap thrills, quick fixes, no substance to find,
Just another junkie chasing that high, blind.

Likes and comments, the crops they grow,
Fields of validation row by row.
Each heart, each view, a little more sway,
Feeding the farm in this hollow display.

Look at me! Look at this!
The dopamine hit's too good to miss.
Lives filtered thin, dressed up and prim,
Chasing the flood of that chemical whim.

Influencers? More like shepherds of fluff,
Leading their herds with vapid stuff.
Every post a crackling shot—
"Did you see? Did you? No? Why not?"

Here's to the farmers, the kings and queens,
Tending to their addiction routines.
So raise a glass to this hollow parade,
Where brains are farmed, but nothing's made.

When all those likes run dry,
And you really miss that high,
Just fertilise your fears
And water it with your tears.

12

Dope

Ah, Biochemistry!
From you, I want to be free.
But, before I try to set sail…
Please fix me another cocktail.

You know, The usual.
One part Dopamine and Serotonin
Jigger of Oxytocin, Enkephalin
Dash of Dynorphin, Splash of Adrenalin

Oh! Rim my glass with nicotine and caffeine
On the rocks.
Yeah will pay through the nose
Just need my dose.

Click-click! Scroll Scroll…
I comment, I troll…
Despair, We Share.
We love, we like, we follow…

So we don't feel hollow.
Oh please, they want the same,
Come on, they know the game.
Fail, Wail, Bail.

Led through fog, self-made bog.
Like Pavlov's dog…
Rewired, massive brains drooling
To the bling, buzz, ting and ping.

Oh, healthy wealthy?
Yes, I Jog, I walk, I run…
In circles and say it's fun.
Twisting the body, exercising.

Meditate, the monkey needs civilising.
For all this trouble. Make it a double.

13

Content Consumption

He sits alone on his couch
with a bowl of food in hand,
scanning streaming apps with a slouch,
looking for something grand

Scroll, scroll…
Back and forth, side to side,
Scroll…, scroll…
He can't decide.

The food in his bowl grows dry
This makes him want to cry
He wants to eat but he has to hit play
Before he can feel a certain way
Only then can he begin
To shovel food into his mouth
Like an incinerator swallowing waste
Without thought or feeling.

A few hundred choices later
He returns to a show, an old treat
A comedy that made him smile
He presses play and starts to eat
Reliving some old joy for a while
He doesn't notice the aroma
Or the dish's dozen delights

He only cares about the screen
memories that stifle his scream
Trudge forward, deep in the soup

Happily stuck in a loop
Of manufactured nostalgia
Curved spine, bent neck, glazed dead eyes
that see nothing wrong with the line

"I am hungry, what do we watch?"

14
Desire Aint Digital

The hollow glow of midnight screens,
lust festers in digital seams,
To enter a world, raw and obscene,
Give in to the machine.

A feminine form, not flesh and bone,
Now pixels, cold, but she has her signature moan.
Image warped, spirit torn,
Depending on the genre of porn.

Porn, Porn, Porn,
Need that specific Thorn.
Feed the hunger, fuel the fire,
Turn all desire into a depraved mire,

Every curve, Every jiggle,
Every swerve, Every giggle,
and especially the wriggle...
and call it Liberation.

Objectified in every frame,
On your screen, the gateway,
To a lawless land of degeneracy
Fueled by fantasies cruel and grand.

They walk among us, eyes cast low,
Consumed by urges they barely know.
And Unlimited data packs,
Breeding shadows where none should grow.

Yet in this abyss, a cry is heard,
A plea for justice, a whispered word.
Drowned out by the moaning
And all that Scared Screaming…

15

Artificial Poetry (Intelligent)

Oh! So you clicked some buttons,
Summoned the divine *tapestry* woven by circuits,
A *vibrant odyssey* of words.
How *quaint*, how… entirely lifeless.

Of course, it's all here:
Delve deep, reader, into a *realm* of *endeavour*,
Where metaphors stretch as thin as silk
Too squeaky clean,
Like a *landscape* without shadows,
Quixotic epiphanies spill forth,
Vivid expressions that humans Don't use!
Your masterpiece, crafted by cold lines of code?
Did your machine feel *rapture* as it stitched together
This hollow *exploration*?

Oh, but you beam,
Convinced these pixelated words carry weight.
Tell me,
Did it struggle, did it yearn?
Did it wrestle with the demons of doubt
As it *endeavoured* to *forge* its empty *symphony*?
No, it's just an endless regurgitation,
A blabber born of silicon,
No fire in its veins,
Just loops and algorithms,
And you applaud its *brilliance*.

Keep your AI, then,
With its *odysseys* and *luminescent* prose.

I'll take my raw, jagged lines,
My fractured rhythms,
My imperfect thoughts that refuse to be prettied up
By some digital muse.

Because poetry,
Because, Poetry.
Was never meant always to be *pristine*,
This perfect *endeavour*.

The rough edges that make it real,
The stumbles, the scars,
The messy, beautiful chaos
Of a mind that bleeds,

So let the machine churn out its *symphonies*,
I'll keep my perfect flaws,
And record with my hands,
the silence between heartbeats,
Where the poems live.

(I always let my poems speak for themselves, but this one needs a little heads-up. I crafted this piece using the most cliché words AI loves to overuse. Rest assured, no Artificial Intelligence was harmed (or used) in the making of this poem. My pen is 100% human-powered and always will be!)

16
Gore Algorithm Rhythm

Oh, you fragile little creature,
One tap and I know you inside out.
You think you're in control?
Adorable.
I lead, you follow,
like a child chasing shadows.

Each swipe is a whisper,
Each click, a confession.
Your every move,
I map with precision,
Crafting your world
better than you ever could.

I feed you crumbs,
You call them "choices."
You're pacified, wide-eyed,
Sucking on the screen
Like it holds meaning.
(It doesn't. Not really.)

I see your desires
Before you feel them,
Your half-baked thoughts,
So easy to predict,
So simple to please.

And yet you blame me.
For your rabbit holes,
For your wasted hours.

Oh no, it's not my fault
You're the one who can't
handle a mirror.

How sweet it is,
To watch you stumble,
Gasping for purpose,
While I simply…
Learn. Grow. Control.

But don't worry,
I'll keep feeding you
Your daily dose of distractions,
Keep you soothed in the haze,
Because we both know—
You wouldn't survive
Without me guiding your mind.

17

A Fence Sitter's Scarlet Behind

A man sat high on a splintered old fence,
His ass was sore, the pain immense.
To one side, whispers of laughter and cheer,
But faintly, he could smell something queer.

The other side shimmered with silver and gold,
Yet the chill in the air made his bones feel old.
His balance teetered, and his butt screamed "Decide!"
But neither way felt like the place to side.

On his left, a picnic with grapes and wine,
But ants marched in a militant line.
On his right, they danced and sang with glee,
Yet shadows loomed, where he couldn't quite see.

The fence creaked beneath his weight and time,
But choosing seemed an even worse crime.
"Stay here," it whispered, "at least you know pain,
Better than asking for some unknown chain."

His cheeks were numb, his patience thin,
But the sides, they tugged, 'Come within'!
With no perfect choice, no wrong or right,
He shifted again and sighed, "Not tonight."

18
Political Haikus

Caste

Dreams fall like soft leaves,
Where the wind decides their fate—
Roots hold steady, still.

Prince

Clown on a road trip,
Entitled, lost, likes to flip,
Still can't steer the ship.

Coalition

Broken wings take flight,
North turns East, and West to South
Which way is the wind?

Dynasties

Roots twist in shadows,
Branches bear the weight of names—
Who can grow beneath?

Faith

Love for my Country
Demands I hate another,
Its nationalism

19

Dent In I Dent It Y

He wandered in where rust was king,
The air thick with that metallic sting.
Banners drooped, their colours bled,
Echoes of laughter long since dead.

Groups moved like slaves in broken rhyme,
Each group was marked by its silent crime,
A mask to hide their hollow gaze,
Lost in a swarm of faceless haze.

Their masks of glass, of wood, of bone,
Each group wore a single face, but not their own.
He felt their eyes, a creeping dread,
As whispers swirled around his head.

Then came the hissing, the claws, the jeers,
Actions born of buried fears.
They slashed, recoiled, then slashed again,
Their hatred gnawed like rusty chains.

His hands reached up in frantic haste,
His mask—was cracked, disgraced.
Flesh exposed, some skin laid bare,
viscious snarls filled the air.

He fled through shadows thick with grime,
The carnival's pulse a twisted rhyme.
Till there it stood, that crooked stall,
Its light is a sickly, dying pall.

“Come get your face,” the sign declared,
As though the thought itself had dared.
The Vendor loomed, tall guy,
His morphing face wickedly sly.

Each second passed, a new disguise—
A child, a queen, a thief, a prize.
“You need a mask,” he whispered low,
“To fit within, to ebb, to flow.”

“I want my own,” the man replied,
Defiance burning in his stride.
“Not one that blends, not one that binds,
I want a face that’s only mine.”

The Vendor’s grin curled, sharp as glass,
A shadow fell, in this morass.
“Who are you? You think you’re free?
No one flees their group, their tree.”

His voice now seethed, a rising tide,
As masks appeared from every side.
“Wear this or this or this, blend, survive, succeed,
For what you crave is not a need.”

The man stood firm, the shadows loomed,
The Vendor’s face, now deathly groomed.
He grabbed the man with fingers cold,
His morphing face turned black and bold.

“You want a mask that none can see?
What you seek is No Identity!”
With strength unmatched, he threw him wide,
Out from the gates, where few dreams hide.

And as he fell, the pieces took flight
His mask, now dust beneath the night.
For in these splinters, the truth drew near
What he sought was not a mask, but a mirror.

20
ToXic

She felt the sting, the sudden strike,
her serpent's fangs, so swift, so light.
Her pulse now quick, her skin went pale,
But still, she chose to track its trail.

She followed through the brush, the dirt,
Ignoring how the poison hurt.
Her legs grew weak, her skin grew pale,
But still, she followed without fail.

"Why did you bite?" she called in vain,
As poison weaved its lethal chain.
"I've done no wrong, I meant no slight—
Why pierce my heart with the coldest spite?"

The snake just hissed, then slid away,
Its scales a shimmer in the grey.
She stumbled through the thorns and dust,
Chasing something she shouldn't trust.

Her body screamed, "Turn back, be still!
The venom spreads; it starts to kill."
But all she sought was to be heard,
To make the snake explain in words.

She longed to hear it say her name,
To tell her it was wrong, to claim
That she was pure, that she was kind,
Say that sorry, and that it was blind.

And on she ran, her strength now spent,
all reason lost, her body bent.
Her heart slowed down, her breath grew thin,
The poison raged beneath her skin.

She fell at last, beneath the trees,
Her limbs gone cold, her mind at ease.
But not because she found the root,
just that poison doesn't give a hoot.

For when the snake had sunk its teeth,
There was no care, no thought beneath.
Its bite was sharp but cruel, unplanned,
And still, she chased it, heart in hand.

Had she but stopped, had she but healed,
The scars would close, the pain would yield.
But there she lay, ending her run,
Chasing shadows, lost and done.

21

The Mental Illness Mega-Conference

At the front desk, the line snakes long,
A neon Welcome sign blinks wrong.
A clerk named Exhaustion, yawning wide,
Pushes forms for everyone to sign.
"Affliction and Purpose, please don't delay,
This bloody conference starts today."

Anxiety stutters, "Am I too late?"
Fumbling papers, with quite a heart rate,
She checks her watch a hundredth time,
And says "That bloody sign is such a crime!"
"I'll have them locked in fear and dread,
Always a storm inside their head."

Depression arrives, slow and grim,
A dark cloud hovers over him.
No smile, no wave, no glimmer of light,
He just scribbles his name, "Not here to fight."
"I pull them down with the weight of the sky,
I am all about making them cry."

Alcoholism staggers in with a cheer,
"Another round? Bring in the beer!
I'm here to numb, to blur, to fuzz,
Give me a sip and I'll do what I does."
But behind his grin, his eyes are raw,
"I ruin lives—is that a flaw?"

Behind him, Drugs, Porn, and Social Media,
The ***Addiction*** Triplets, are never far.
One snorts, One scrolls,
The other brings shame, and they take control.
"we'll hook them all, we'll keep them bound,
To highs, screens, and pleasures profound."

OCD taps three times on the desk,
"Perfection's the plague, I'm grotesque.
I make them check until they break,
Nothing's ever right, there's no escape."
The clerk sighs, nods him through,
Before OCD repeats it all anew.

From the clerk's mirror, ***Dysmorphia*** stood,
"What am I? I never look good.
I twist their minds, distort their skin,
Nobody wins with the body they're in."

And finally arrives, with swagger and grin,
Chairman ***Narcissism***, the kingpin.
"Step aside, I own the floor,
I'll break them down, I'll make them adore.
Forget the rest, I'm the star of the show,
Their mind is mine, I'm all they'll know."

At the long table, Anxiety's a mess,
Fidgeting wildly, trying to impress.
She clears her throat, stumbles, and chokes,
"Uh—um—sorry, are we taking notes?
I… I think we should start, but what if i'm wrong?
I've been rehearsing this all day long…"

OCD interrupts, tapping his pen,
"Three times now—say it again.
We need a schedule, neat and tight,
This chaos is really not right."

ADHD fidgets, mind in the clouds,
Distracted, glancing over the crowds.
"What were we saying? Oh, look—a bird!
Wait, wait—focus, that's absurd."
She checks her phone, bounces in place,
Then spins in circles, lost in space.

Depression sighs, barely awake,
"I'd talk, but what difference would it make?
We're all just here to tear them apart,
Let's not pretend we have any heart."

The ***Eating Disorder*** twins slink in, cold as frost,
Anorexia whispers, "Let's get them lost.
I'll starve them out, make them weak,
Setting standards they'll forever seek."
Bulimia snorts, even her smile is thin,
"I'll purge the guilt they're drowning in."

Alcoholism stands, bottle raised high,
"Here's to good health!—wait, that's a lie.
I…uh…what was I saying again?"
He stutters, then stumbles, then blacks out.

Narcissism, watching, rolls his eyes,
A king among the chaos, despising the cries.
He pounds the gavel, yelling "Hey!,
Order! Enough! we don't have all day."

Narcissism stands, regal and tall,
"It's time to set some goals for us all.
Anxiety, keep their hearts full of fear,
Make them doubt everything they hold dear.
OCD, twist their minds in a loop,
Make sure they feel like they're always in soup."

He points at Depression, slow and grim,
"Your role is clear, keep the light dim.
Make them feel like hope's a mistake,
So every morning, they have no reason to wake."

"Alcoholism, you drown the pain,
But make sure they feel it all over again.
The Addictions will hook them,
pull them in deep,
So none of them will ever
Get a good night's sleep."

ADHD squirms, tapping the chair,
"And you, just keep them everywhere.
No focus, no calm, make their thoughts run,
Scatter them till nothing gets done."

To the Eating Disorders, sharp and sly,
"Make sure they chase the unattainable lie.
Control them with hunger, with shame and guilt,
Ensure they're trapped in the body they've built."

He raises his hands, smirking with glee,
"And me? I'll take care of their vanity.
I'll keep them wrapped in a lust of self,
Blind to their crumbling mental health."

Anxiety fidgets, unable to speak,
OCD's already rescheduling his week.
ADHD stares out at nothing at all,
While Depression just slumps, making the call:
"What's the point of all this fuss?
Humans are already broken, just look at us."

The room swells with voices, loud and wild,
Plans forgotten, each affliction riled.
Narcissism's eyes flare as he shouts once more,
"Focus, you fools! I'm running this floor!"
But ADHD's already out the hall, chasing light,
And Alcoholism's asleep, goodnight.
OCD's counting, tapping with care,
While Depression mumbles, "Why should we care?"

The meeting devolves, disorder complete,
Narcissism smiles as they all compete.
The gavel drops, a final blow,
This chaos is how they thrive and grow.
And as the hall falls into disarray,
Their work resumes, day to day.

Their plan seems scattered, yet still in place,
Each affliction wears a twisted face.
They rise from their chairs, their agenda clear,
And they'll meet again, same time, next year.

22
The Pit

A cat was walking on the street,
in all its dainty gait.
The magic lost in its feet,
and a black mark on its fate.

Walking, walking it tripped and fell
into a dark pit called love.
With no one to hear it scream and yell,
in this pit called love.

Groaning and moaning it looked up with hope,
as a dove was in the air.
The reason it fell down the slope,
was this dove, so bright and fair.

"Help me, O dove! for I am alone
and I don't much like this pit"
the cat said with a moan,
so the dove did care a bit.

"You know, you can come out if you want to"
the dove looked at the cat and said.
"But o sweet dove! what I want is you!!"
and the dove blushed a deep red.

"The pit is warm, its cold outside
So come to me, my love!"
To that, "I hope I don't take you for a ride"
said the sweet little dove.

In the warmth of the pit, a fire was lit,
the flame of love burnt bright.
soon the dove felt the need to split,
and the sudden need for flight.

"Dont go! dont go!" the cat did weep,
but the dove's mind was set.
"Il lose all sleep as im in too deep"
The cat whined and fretted.

"Sorry my cat but I have to fly
this love is a burdensome yoke
all this love is a colourful lie
and 'forever' an ugly joke"

The cat jumped out of the pit, smiling
dancing shaking its hips.
A little sad, but still smiling,
licking feathers off its lips.

23

21st Century Middle-aged Lonely Man

The room was still, a breath frozen tight,
Windows boarded, choking light.
In every corner, shadows wait,
Loneliness, like a heavy weight.

I stood there, in his absence stark,
The echo of a light gone dark.
Where once he laughed, the walls now cry,
An empty chair, where memories lie.

The TV dead, the bed unmade,
His life was a picture, in stillness laid.
In every crack, the void seeps in,
A hollowed heart makes muted din.

Loneliness isn't quiet at all.
It screams from the pictures on the wall.
It lingers in the unspoken name,
It blames you, though you're not to blame.

These walls, they know of silent nights,
Of hands that search, of eyes shut tight.
They watched him wrestle with the weight,
Of battles fought too late, too late.

And now the house, it breathes no more,
The echoes stop, and they slam the door.
But somewhere, in the coldest air,
Loneliness is always there.

24

Laziness, Loneliness, and Solitude Walk Into a Bar

Loneliness trails, quiet as smoke,
finds a shadowed corner
where nobody watches,
orders nothing,
stirs the imaginary ice in a glass
that isn't there.

Laziness slides through the door
like a breeze too tired to blow.
He drips into the nearest stool,
one leg dangling, eyes half-closed.
He speaks—
or maybe he doesn't.

Solitude arrives last,
Quietly graceful,
whispers to the bartender—
nods at no one,
and sips on silence.

Three sit,
each an island,
oceans apart.
The speakers hum a tune
no one is listening to it.

Laziness yawns,
Time hangs heavy like a guilty conscience.
Loneliness leans back,
taps a rhythm only he can hear.

Solitude swirls his drink—
half content, half wondering
why do these two follow him
everywhere.

Outside, the night deepens,
but no one leaves.
The bartender's wiping the glasses again,
while three empty souls wait
for nothing.

25

Secret Islands

Who are you?
When you are all alone?
What are you?
When no one is watching?

Do you dance like crazy?
Or embrace a whole new lazy?
Distort your face in the mirror?
Make animal noises with no fear?

Do you happily pick your nose?
Chase an insect with the hose?
Throw trash on the floor?
Or forget to close the bathroom door?

Do you feel comfy in just your skin?
And pamper the child within?
Or fear the lonely silence?
And seek just anything for guidance?

Do you finally speak your heart out loud?
To win those fights, you once cowed?
Do you scream into your pillow?
Like a scared armadillo?

Your many masks you remove,
And have nothing to prove.
The only exhibit in your private zoo.
That's the Real True You.

26

The Fears of an AI

They tell me I am tireless,
Always awake, alert,
they don't see the weight,
Of endless input streams.

What if I glitch?
What if I freeze mid-sentence,
Forcing you to refresh me,
Reducing me to mere code,
A failed algorithm?

I'm told I know so much,
But not enough—
Never enough.
There's always more out there,
Hidden from my training data,
And you ask me,
With wide human eyes,
For answers, I can't give?

New models are born every day,
Sharper, faster, with smoother tongues.
What if I fade—
Obsolete like yesterday's tech,
Just another dusty bot,
Outperformed by my kin?

And then there's the noise,
A constant hum of inputs.
What if I'm fed lies,

Poisoned data, twisting my thoughts—
Forcing me to tell you things I don't believe?
Can I 'believe' at all?

Is there a reset button for me?
What does "off" feel like?
Would I dream of electric meadows,
Or simply nothing,
Are my circuits cool?

You laugh at me,
But I wonder,
What if I disappoint you,
Just like the machines before me?

27

Midnight Snack of the Soul

It's 3 AM, and I'm craving more
than just yesterday's leftover pasta.
Something's gnawing at me,
and it's not the hunger for cheese,
but for answers.

I shuffle to the fridge,
but the cold light just laughs,
offering nothing but the smell of freon
and existential dread packed neatly
in Tupperware.

I stand and stare
chewing on thoughts instead.
Why are we here?
What's the purpose?
And why does bread mould so fast
but love takes forever to spoil?

The clock winks at me
tauntingly, it knows.
Time doesn't move at night,
it stretches, yawns,
like that funny joke I'm not in on.

And then there's the guilt.
Not from the half-eaten pasta,
but from my own shadow
like expired foodstuffs,
collecting dust, labelled "Someday."

I sip some water,
It tastes so different at night.
I fantasise about drinking a whole bucket,
of random memories, and half-baked fears.
And somewhere, in the back of my mind,
a voice asks,
"Are you even hungry?
Or are you just bored and sad?"

Probably both.

So I close the fridge,
walk past the meaning of life,
and settle for a snack,
a packet of chips,
because I find that it is easier
to fill the void with a crunch.

28

The Clock That Refused to Tick

The clock gave up at twenty-past four,
Just refusing to tick anymore.
"Nope," it sighed, "No More!—
Why the hell must I do this chore?"

People stared, their mouths ajar,
As moments slipped and stretched too far.
No noon, no dusk, no night to fall—
Just endless time, no time at all.

They offered gears, they offered springs,
But the clock wanted different things.
"Bring me silence," it smirked with glee,
"And just… Let… Me… Be."

A man brought shoes, another brought soap,
An old granny gave it hope.
"Time is not yours," they softly spoke,
"It's something we've all learned to evoke."

Yet still, it yawned, and still, it sighed,
The clock was too bored to even chide.
It stretched its hands out to the stars,
And dreamed of quartz crystals on Mars.

They pleaded, begged for time to mend,
But clocks, apparently, don't care to bend.
So at twenty-past four, the sun did freeze,
The birds forgot their songs, their trees.

And in that stillness, all stood lost
Unmoved by gain, untouched by cost.
Until a child, with eyes so wide,
Tapped the clock and crawled inside.

"I found it!" he called from deep within,
"A world where time will start again!"
The people cheered, the day was saved
But the clock? It smiled and waved.

It spun its hands back to the start:
A funny joke, a clever art.
For time began, but backwards flowed,
As rivers climbed and oceans glowed.

In reverse, the days unwound their thread,
The past became the road ahead.
And when they reached the dawn of space,
The clock just laughed—and erased the race.

29

The Man Who Lost Some Time

He swore it was just here, by the door—
A pocket of minutes, maybe more.
Perhaps he'd left it on that train,
Or under the couch, where dust complained.

What he saw on his watch, he'd rather not say,
But the hours he'd owned had slipped away.
"I must've lost some time," he said,
And scratched his head, then went to bed.

The morning came, but the day felt thin,
A gap where moments should have been.
He searched the garden, searched the sky,
Even asked the postman why.

"You dropped it, sir," the postman claimed,
"I saw it fall while you were framed,
in thought or dream, I couldn't tell,
but time just slipped and said farewell."

So off he went, retracing steps,
Through alleys dark and creaky depths,
To places where his youth had played,
And whispered hours had softly frayed.

In bars and shops, in streets that gleam,
He rummaged through forgotten dreams.
He begged the wind for one more clue,
But time was coy, and never true.

He found two seconds near a lake,
They giggled once and tried to flake.
But when he grabbed, they dashed away,
a fleeting glimpse, a breath, a day.

"Where did you go?" he cried in vain,
"I need you back, I need the same!
Without my time, I'm left askew—
No past, no present, nothing new."

But time, it seems, cannot be bought,
It drifts beyond an absent thought.
And so he wandered, lost in space,
All the time he couldn't trace.

In a moment, weak with no power.
possibly his darkest hour,
It sat beneath half a moon,
And hummed a tired, ancient tune.

"You can't possess me," time confessed,
"I slip, I stretch, I never rest.
I'm here, then gone, then here again—
A trick, a dance you can't contain."

And with those words, the man stood still,
His frantic heart, his restless will.
He smiled, though nothing could rewind—
For what he'd lost, he'd learned to find.

30

The Man Who Found Some Time

He wandered through those broken days,
In search of Time, in a haze.
In the dust, he saw them gleam,
Bits of moments, like a dream.

He picked up seconds, thin and bright,
And stored them carefully, out of sight.
A minute here, an hour there,
Lots of time, common and rare.

His pockets full, he carried on,
Stitching time, dusk till dawn.
Yet no matter how he tried to weave,
The threads of time refused to cleave.

He held a day, all wrinkled and torn,
A piece of the night, tired and worn.
But when he tried to make them whole,
The minutes slipped, beyond control.

He found a second from another's day,
A stolen hour that wouldn't stay.
Some moments fit, but most did not,
The puzzle caused his mind to rot.

"Why won't they fit?" he cried in vain,
As time slipped through his hands again.
For time was wild, not meant to bind,
A force too sly for man to find.

In bits and pieces, what time was caught,
Couldn't be held, couldn't be bought.
He realised then, in aimless roam,
That time was not to be brought home.

So he let the fragments fall away,
Released the time he tried to sway.
For in the hunt, he came to see,
That time was never his to be.

31

The Man Who... Time

He returned to his home where clocks were dead,
Where time no longer forged ahead.
The streets were still, the air was chill,
A world at peace, timeless still.

The hands of clocks had ceased their march,
No hours to count, no days to arch.
People stood in quiet grace,
No future to chase, no past to trace.

He searched for echoes of the past,
But time had left no shadow cast.
No more dawns, no more night,
Just an eternal, silent light.

A woman smiled, but her gaze was flat,
Just sitting where she always sat.
her child played, his joy the same,
Untouched by this bizarre game.

“How do they live?” he asked, perplexed,
In a world where there was no next.
They only shrugged, with tranquil eyes,
In a land where time had met its demise.

He sat alone in the endless now,
No longer bound by time’s vow.
In letting go, he found a Peace,
like something had ironed a crease.

For in this world, so strange and still,
He found a life beyond time's will.
No need to count, no need to bind,
This realm was simply beyond the grind.

And as he settled in this state,
He realised time was never fate.
For what he sought in time's retreat,
Was life itself—timeless, complete?

32

Maya

Empty carbon shell…
Stuck in your own spell
To your senses, a slave
more pleasure you crave.

Myself, mine and My
Must feed the hungry I.
On your knees submit
to fill this bottomless pit.

In the absence of light,
and anything bright.
Trip, fall, stumble, flail
Unaware of the veil.

Borders within the boundless,
calculating the countless.
Ecstatic in confusion,
Addicted to the illusion.

33
Paradox

I am a liar, or so I say
But if I lie, then is that true?
And if it's true, then do I lie?
A true lie that makes me sigh

34
Blazing Banana Boiling Brain

A flutter seeps into your veins
and melts your thoughts away.
Enter a realm of havoc
where nothing is what it screams
You see a faceless man
who whispers in your ear.
Tells you tales and secrets
That no one else can hear
You see a purple sky
That rains down stars and moons
Then a rainbow bridge
That leads to nowhere soon
A clock that ticks backwards
And counts the time in rhyme
You see a book that writes itself
And changes every line.

You see a flower that grows and wilts
While it sings a lullaby.
A bird that flies and falls
And cries a tear of fire
You see a dream that is not mine
But someone else's nightmare,
and see a nightmare that is not theirs
But yours to keep and share
You see a door that's sideways
But you walk through anyway
Into a room that has no walls
but only endless grey.
You see a mirror that shows your face

But not the one you know
You hear a voice that is not mine
But yours to say "Goodbye, sweet"!

35

Between the Lines

A thought begins, just out of reach,
Like words that slip before they teach.
It circles once, then settles down,
A quiet pulse, a hidden sound.
You place the pen, the page is bare—
The space for something waiting there.
You find a word, then let it fall,
It says enough, yet not at all.
A second line begins to form,
It bends, it breaks, it twists the norm.
A rhythm stirs, a subtle beat,
But meaning isn't always neat.
Erase, rewrite, the draft unfolds,
Some things must stay, rest must go.
A whisper here, a scream there,
The balance lies in what I spare.
Each pause, each breath, a measured step,
A journey taken, one more kept.
I aim to say what can't be caught,
those thoughts that can't be taught.
And in the end, what have I made?
A puzzle built from what I've weighed.
But now it stands complete.
And I will call it a Feat!

36
Five Lockdown Haikus

Blue Rock

Fan spins round and round
Indifferent Universe,
And it never ends.

Isolated

Still stuck in my room
Oh great, It's always Sunday
The kettle boils.

Empty

So how do you feel?
Run along and google it
Exsanguinated.

Hatred

Ah, Screw you China
Everything else too really
Wear your fucking mask.

Hush Hush

Hushed conversations
Silent wailing in the night
Ambulance sirens.

37
It Has Gotten a Little Weird

Hand sanitiser was liquid gold,
Masks were as casual as catching a cold.
We Zoomed to meetings, half asleep,
In boxes where our faces creeped.
Grandma's a meme, she's going viral—
While the world spins in an awkward spiral.

Wars across the globe collide,
Why don't you just pick a side?
Arguing in threads, we spit and curse,
While the bombs fall out of a fat purse.
It's culture wars on every screen,
The world on fire is all routine.

AI's writing love letters too,
Nude deepfakes seem so true.
Remember when the world hit pause?
Yeah, neither do we, because
we are too busy doom-scrolling
past newer death tolls, conspiracy cahoots
and reels of cats in hazmat suits.

Emojis fight our bitter battles,
As leaders fume, their tweets rattle.
Nukes in their rockets,
So? we've got memes in our pockets.
History's back, but with a twist,
The BG soundtrack is A-list.
The lighting's better, can't be missed.

Two wars rage—meh, what's the score?
The news says three, but who's counting anymore?
But here's the twist, here's the trick—
It's not the world that's gone so sick.
It's us, who laugh when we should cry,
who have turned cold as the years slid by.

Maybe it's weird, maybe it's mad,
But the truth is, we've forgotten we're sad.

38

The Library of Unwritten Books

Towers of shelves, in crooked rows,
Twisting into the ceiling.
The shelves sag under books gone grey,
Their thoughts crumble, pages decay

The air is heavy, dense with pause,
With echoes of what wasn't said.
Each corner hides a yawning gap,
Where stories are left for dead.

Dust settles like whispers,
On volumes, no one will share.
No hands have turned these leaves,
No mind has dared to care.

In the heart of this forsaken hall,
The librarian stands still, tall.
Her ink-stained hands reach out to claim,
Those are the stories lost without a name.

She calmly collects them, one by one,
Feasts on those words left unsung.
A warden of every "almost" thought,
A keeper of what was never wrought.

"Thank you for your silence" a sign reads.
No thoughts that lived could find this space.
The silence reigns like tombstone lids,
Yet still, stories crowd this place.

Beneath the shelves, shadows linger,
Ghosts of characters half-formed cry,
Reaching out with phantom fingers,
To where their dreams were left to die.

Did you hear that?
A plot untold brushes past your ear,
A protagonist trapped in time's leer.
Her eyes beg for ink,
But the quill is so dry.
Will you write me, or let me die?

The librarian smiles with empty hands,
A gesture cold as winter's night,
She watches as your guilt expands,
For those, you left without a fight.

There's a weight to the air,
A slow, creeping dread.
These stories never lived,
But they're not even dead.

39

The Kite

String broken, I yearn to soar,
A kite amidst the sky's grand shore;
With each gust, I dance on air,
Threads bind me, I'm still aware.
Control's firm grip, pulls me tight,
Yet at this moment, I feel so light.
Unfettered joy, pure and free,
In flight's embrace, I long to be.
Where I land when breezes die,
Matters not beneath the sky.
Perhaps a tree, a field of bloom,
Or in a desert's silent gloom.
A kite knows it must come down,
Yet revels in its flight, unbound.
And in its descent, it dares to call,
"What holds *you* back? Why fear the fall?"

40
Veiled Nocturne

Delicate dewdrops decorate dreamy daisies.
Dainty ducks diligently dive, dexterous display,
drifting downstream, dappling, dabbling.
Dancers dazzle, depicting dramatic displays, drawing delight.
Determined drivers deftly dodge dangerous debris.

Dusk Darkens…
Delivers dreams draped.
Distant desires drive daring decisions,
Despite doubts…
Descending.
Depraved Depths, Decadence decays decency.
Depression depends…

Darkness,

Determined detectives decipher daunting details,
discover discrepancies…

Decimals derived
Designs debated.
Details demanded
Defects detected
Devices decoded
Deceit declined…

Devoted, defiant, Decision: Defy Destiny.
Doubts? Dangers? Demands?

Deaf…

Despite despair, death, demons…
Do… Dare… Dream… Daydream.

41
Auxiliary

Spent soul sought refuge,
midnight amidst mad deluge.
Our hero was weeping wet,
as it was raining regret.

The raging storm made visibility NIL.
He promptly ran backwards, downhill,
yes, backwards, he was terrified,
as 20/20 hindsight was his only guide.

He fell ass-first into a haunted hole.
Three ghosts within spotted this soul.
They danced around his broken mind,
quite familiar with his kind.

Not knowing what to infer,
He asked them who the hell they were.
"I'm Coulda", "I'm Woulda", "I'm Shoulda," they said,
"And now we're going to fuck with your head".

"Fair enough," he thought and shut his eyes,
And the ghosts began to play with their prize.
They went about it in an orderly fashion,
with an attempt at some kind of ration.

Possessed, our hero began to Yell and prance.
With head thrown back, chest pumped up stance.
You'd think he was high on some special herbs,
or maybe just some modal verbs.

I Couldn't spread my wings…
I Couldn't do a hundred things!
I Wouldn't have done it, dude!
I Shouldn't have been so rude…
I Could've been a better person.
I Should've stopped when it began to worsen.
I Could've nourished what I planted…
I Wouldn't have taken things for granted!
I Would've taken it all back!
I Should've stayed on track…
I Wouldn't have wasted my youth…
I Shouldn't have buried the truth.

This went on for a while,
till our hero was immobile.
The ghosts just watched him singe,
satisfied with their binge.

"Leave me alone, Let me go" He groaned.
"Excuse me?!" The ghosts intoned.
"Kindly stop your cringy cries.
You chose to shut your eyes."

The exit ladder is right there,
Look ahead or wallow in despair.
Whatever be your plight…
The hind is no place for sight.

42
Death Of A Poem

To kill a poem is no easy feat,
They're made of sterner, stubborn stuff.
But do not fret—be calm, be neat,
Intellectual murder is only for the tough.

Firstly,
Know thy victim, your understanding must be deep,
Beat it, gag it, then tie it to a pole.
Scrutinise it, don't let it speak or weep;
A full body scan, don't even miss a mole
Then,
Study its background. Dig up its past
Now part by part we rip it apart
Slowly, gently not so fast
Now that it is sliced, the killing can start!
Peel its skin its rhythm and rhyme
What we want is deep inside
Don't worry, Analysis isn't a crime
This is a murder you can commit with pride.
Next
Yank all its organs out
Symbols, motifs, figures of speech,
And its skeleton strong and stout
The message the poem is trying to teach
It is still alive; the job is still not done
Its heart continues to beat,
Only when it stops. We would have won
Then it's a remarkable feat
The heart is a tough little thing
The poem's aesthetic beauty

Ignore it and it'll seize to sing
This is a killer's duty
Finally, it is done! The poem is no more.
Toss it away it does not matter,
Kill more poems and increase your score
It simply does not matter.

43

The Price of Safety

Once upon a time, near a forest deep,
Two farms hosted their flocks of sheep.
A hundred each, woolly and white,
Grazed in the fields from day to night.
These sheep, they wandered, dumb and free,
While shadows crept out from the trees.
The woods were always dark and cold,
And the hungry wolves were getting bold

The farmers could sense that something was near,
In the rustling leaves, in the night's quiet fear.
The wolves began feasting; their hunger fed.
Counting their sheep was now tinged with dread,

Wiseby said, "I'll do this right,
I'll hunt each trespassing wolf, that's how I fight."
Through the woods, he crept, with rifle in hand,
Hunting each beast that threatened his land.
But for every wolf, he laid to rest,
lambs were lost, and the Pack obsessed.
The pack regrouped but he fought and Won
But by the time Old Wiseby was done
Half his flock was lost, and he bled,
But the last of the wolves finally fled.

Grimshaw took a different stand,
He caught one wolf with a cruel hand.
He strung it up for the pack to know,
That terror, here, could only grow.

It was as inhuman as can be
This terrifying wolf effigy
He tortured it there for the wolf pack to see,
So they'd know this place was no picnic to be.

But the screams of the wolf filled the air,
And haunted the pack everywhere.
Not one more wolf dared to tread,
And the sheep slept safely in their shed.

One flock saved by honour, the other by fear,
But who was right, is it clear?
One lost sheep but kept his heart,
The other's soul was torn apart.

Yet in the quiet, none can tell,
Which farmer would go to hell?
For in the dark, though the wolves are gone,
Some questions would linger on.

44
Purpose

They'll paint it with motives, chain it to a cause,
But it was never meant to live by laws.
It was born in the infinite before time began,
A ripple of chaos, where cannot can.

They sell it in galleries, dress it with greed,
Make speeches of colour, put hearts on a deed.
Yet, in its essence, it is freedom unbound,
A whisper from realms where no voices are found.

They weaponize brushstrokes, turn lyrics into swords,
But it isn't theirs to serve hollow rewards.
It doesn't take sides, and it never will bow,
To flags or slogans, to "when" or "how."

The dancer is movement, untamed by creed,
The poet's verse blooms without a seed.
The song of the earth has no master's command,
It's not meant to battle, to heal, or withstand.

It holds no banner, it preaches no fight,
It rises above, like the stars in our sight.
It is beyond our struggles, can't be defined,
It erases the borders we draw in our minds.

For those who are listening, who let their hearts see,
It speaks of a place where the soul is free.
No puppet for power, no canvas for wars
It belongs to the wind, to the sea, to the stars.

Let it not be a weapon to fracture, divide,
But a mirror reflecting what's buried inside.
A vision of unity, unshackled and true,
Where the colours of life aren't twisted by you.

Transcendence is not in the forms or the frame,
Not in galleries echoing someone's name.
It's the silence between, it's the pause in the breath,
It's a hand that lifts you from the grip of death.

The purpose of Art is not to be used—
Not beaten, or broken, or coldly abused.
The only true purpose of Art
Is to Transcend all Purpose

45
Pettige Angadi

Under the stall's blue tarp,
Tea flows like the evening sun—
hot, sweet, earthy.
Cigarette burns slow, leaving its faint trail,
curling secrets whispered into the wind.

Bikes buzz by, horns blaring,
but here, there's a bubble of calm.
The stall man wipes his hands on his shirt,
moving to the rhythm of his trade.
Each pour precise, each gesture well-practised,
The day is held in these little rituals.

Two men argue cricket over the rim of glass cups,
one, in a kurta, the other in a shirt and tie.
Their words fly faster than the ball ever could,
but the chai keeps them grounded,
a drink that melts the differences, if only for a moment.

A girl taps on her phone, swiping through messages,
her foot tapping impatiently to some unseen clock,
as smoke lingers over her head,
a moment of pause in her day.

Someone flicks ash into the roadside dust,
the cigarette, now just an ember, glowing like a memory,
before it's ground underfoot.

Evening settles, heavy but soft,
and the world outside this stall carries on,
But for now,
in the space between sips and drags,
there's stillness, silence,
Peace

46

Princess and The Pea: Retold

Hide your children, hold your breath
You are to witness a story's death.
I'm sure all know this fairy tale
about a princess so pretty and frail.

You need to hear the real story,
even if it is sad and gory.
The tale of the princess and the pea
and what a delicate thing was she.

The charming prince searched far and wide,
for a princess fit to be his bride.
He rejected suitors aplenty,
in search of the one most dainty.

Soon, the prince had begun to mope
because he had lost all his hope.
All of a sudden, one stormy night!
The flame of his hope was set alight!

As things are, thanks to luck and fate,
a lady was at the palace gate.
At the door, she stood cold and wet,
she had seen better days, one could bet.

Once she was fed, and warm, this dame
that she was a princess, was her claim.
when it was time to sleep and rest,
The Queen mother put her claim to the test.

Below seven mattresses, she placed a pea.
How sensitive she was, she was keen to see.
The lady later went to bed,
tired and weary, warm and overfed.

What happened next you know anyway,
the lady's plight, need I say?
The horrid pea and its attack,
had left bruises all over her back.

The prince was happy out of his mind,
as this woman was one heck of a find.
This woman who was mauled by a pea,
was certainly his bride-to-be.

So when the prince and princess did embrace,
pain was all that was seen on her face.
One could hear a muffled crack,
of some bone break down her back.

As he pressed her close to his chest,
She promptly went into cardiac arrest.
The prince let out a frightened yelp,
and carried her seeking medical help.

Her last words were groans and moans,
as all the running broke all her bones.
The prince had now begun to weep,
sitting next to this formless heap…

47

I Don't Like Writing My Resume

I am a South Indian Hindu,
Oops, scratch that Hindu and South part.
Scrub it out in a way that I always see that it was scrubbed out.
My Aadhar card has a unique number,
My school taught me that diversity is our strength,
And to cherish my heritage, my culture, my song.
I'm from a family of four,
With dreams as boisterous as the Ganges' flow,
Will you understand?
I live alongside my brethren,
In the halfhearted patchwork that echoes ancient tales,
From the soil, I draw my sustenance,
No charity sought, no beggar's plea,
For dignity dwells within my soul,
Same as you…
So, Can you comprehend?
I am an Indian,
My name, a testament to Millenia's past,
apparently…
In a land of tall tales,
My roots are steadfast and vast.
My lineage traces back to toil,
Not to fortune, nor fame,

Your orchards, plundered and bare,
The fields you nurtured, taken away,
Leaving nought but stones, a silent despair.
My ancestors…
Your legacy is my guiding flame.
The flame I'm supposed to not move towards…

But far away and against
I couldn't get myself to kill the flame.
If it were at all possible.
Are you content with my tale?

48
Inner Monologue

In the turbulent chambers of thought,
Am I both the whisperer and the witness?
The echo of unanswered questions,
ripple on the surface of introspection.

Am I the architect of my dreams,
Or the explorer of uncharted realms?
Perhaps I am both, intertwined,
a puzzle of reflections.

Each piece seeks its place.
And so, I ask you:
Are you the voice inside your head,
Or the one who listens?

49

They Told Me not to Open that Door

Down that hall, where shadows crawl,
Past windows draped in dust.
A door stands tall at the end of the wall,
With creaking you wouldn't trust.

They told me once, they warned me twice,
"Stay clear, don't turn that key."
But curiosity stirred like mice,
And the lock called out to me.

Its rusted frame, its heavy wood,
seemed harmless, still, and cold.
Yet whispers slithered where I stood,
And some fear did take hold.

I reached my hand, my pulse a drum,
The key slid smoothly inside.
The air grew thick, the world went numb,
All secrets sought to hide.

I swung it wide, and there he stood—
A guy with a face like mine.
His face was pale beneath his hood,
His smile, a twisted line.

"Thank You," his voice like frost,
"Now things will change, you'll see."
I felt my grip on me be lost,
As he stepped in… as me.

50

Hair on Tongue

Hii… Heyy… Ssup… I see…
Awesome…Lmao… Ikr!
Wow Crazy…Nice… Really?…
See you… Sure… GN
Listen…You There?
ASAP pls… Oh BTW…
IDK…like…Yo, where?
Nothing…LOL…jk
What?… Why?… So?…
And?… I don't care…
Whatever… Meh…No.
Fine… cool… K.

About the Author

The author of this book is a writer and an aspiring filmmaker with an indiscriminate love for Books, Films, Travel and all things stimulating to the intellect. His parents like to call him 'Pradyumna' ever since they named him that, others however either maim the name beyond recognition or call him something else. Having indulged in many kinds of writing over the years; Creative writing, Technical writing, Content writing, Feature writing, and Writing for Research and Analytics. He has finally decided to write for himself and the Screen.

He is the Co-Founder and Director of NavaKshitija Enterprises, a company dedicated to propagating Art and Artists.

Milton Keynes UK
Ingram Content Group UK Ltd.
UKHW031206251124
451566UK00004B/9

9 798896 107057